1/11/23
Key West

For Marie, ♡

FERSACE

Poems by

Nicole Tallman

Thank you for the beauty of your words.

With love and gratitude,

Nicole ♡

Copyright © 2023 Nicole Tallman

All rights reserved. No part of this publication may be reproduced, distributed, or transmitted in any form or by any means, including photocopying, recording, or other electronic or mechanical methods, without the prior written permission of the publisher, except in the case of brief quotations embodied in critical reviews and certain other noncommercial uses permitted by copyright law. For permission requests, write to the publisher at the address below.

ELJ Editions, Ltd. is committed to publishing works of quality and integrity. In that spirit, we are proud to offer this poetry collection to our readers. Names, characters, places, and incidents either are the product of the author's imagination or are used fictitiously, and any resemblance to actual persons, living or dead, business establishments, events, or locales is entirely coincidental.

ISBN: 978-1-942004-64-6

Library of Congress Control Number: 2023947527

Cover Design by Laurie Marshall

ELJ Editions, Ltd.
P.O. Box 815
Washingtonville, NY 10992

www.elj-editions.com

Praise for FERSACE

Part cultural satire, part journal intime, part poetic memoir, Nicole Tallman seamlessly stitches these modes of language to take us on her humorous yet serious journey through those proverbial questions of home we all ask ourselves. Replete with evocative imagery, unique metaphors, and a resolute voice, *FERSACE* explores the various geographical, psychological, and natural landscapes that intersect and interact to render our sense of place. A must-read for anyone who grapples with what it means to belong, or not belong, somewhere.

—RICHARD BLANCO, AUTHOR OF *HOW TO LOVE A COUNTRY*

In *FERSACE* (a term she coins for knockoff VERSACE), Nicole Tallman uses the glitz and glamor of Miami, Paris Hilton, and Barbie dolls for reflection about "aging naturally" in our culture of consumerism. Through this lens, she can say anything! She uses the natural world to combat our regressive political times—see, especially, "The Moon is Gay (AKA Say Gay!)". Engaging with the world as well as the personal, Nicole interviews herself in poems written in collaboration with a Ouija board and in others such as "What's it like to live in Miami?" and "What's your Spirit Animal?" Her late mother is a constant in this delightfully female-centric book, with epistolary poems to Sylvia Plath, Lorde, Betty White, and Lana Del Rey. These poems are compelling, funny, and true.

—DENISE DUHAMEL, AUTHOR OF *SECOND STORY*

Between Miami and Michigan, between memory and mourning, *FERSACE* guides us through the vibrant living world of Nicole Tallman's poetry with exactitude and grace. She writes "But I'm no longer sure what I love" and instead of shying away from that thought, Tallman invites us to dive further in and discover what *is* loved as we journey through this wonderful collection.

—ARIEL FRANCISCO, AUTHOR OF *A SINKING SHIP IS STILL A SHIP*

Built on deadpan observations tinged with grief and melancholy, the poems in Nicole Tallman's *FERSACE* train a keen eye on modern day society and tackle everything from the iconography of Barbie, Lorde, and Paris Hilton, urban legends, corporate boardrooms, youth culture, advice via Ouija, and the elusive search for home—brilliantly reduced to the ephemeral waft of a scented candle. Part wink, part takedown, part truth bomb, Tallman's *FERSACE* is a meditation on artifice—how it permeates the personal, the public, the private, the political, and how despite all it tries to conceal, the truth beneath the surface will reveal itself no matter how expertly it is submerged.

—CARIDAD MORO-GRONLIER, AUTHOR OF *TORTILLERA*

Nicole Tallman's *FERSACE* is absolutely magical and bravely human at the same time—tender, funny, canny, with poems that make me so happy this poet is in the world the same time I am, checking it out, letting it in, creating her own myth with a mind like no other, full of surprises and just the perfect word. "In Michigan, they/called me *broad*. In Miami,/they call me *flaca*." The poems in *FERSACE* love the truth. They love the truth in an ocean and they love the truth in a cornfield, and always with an eye on the reader, respecting our visions and journeys, aware of our own wild presence. Tallman shares her words with the heart of a storyteller who knows we have stories to tell as well. "I love everyone who adds to this poem." she says. I love these poems.

—MAUREEN SEATON, AUTHOR OF *THE SKY IS AN ELEPHANT*

Miami's cool. Miami's a place where you can be yourself.
—Gianni Versace

CONTENTS

PROLOGUE

FERSACE	3
POEM FOR PARIS HILTON	4
NOT SEEN	6

I.

FALL	9
RIFLE SEASON	10
DYING YOUNG	11
THE HOLY TRINITY	12
DEAR LORDE:	13
MAMI	14
A WOMAN CALLED MY FACE	15
DEAR BARBIE:	16
FLACA	17
HEMINGWAY DRANK MOJITOS AND OTHER MIAMI MYTHS	18
GRINGA	19
WHAT'S IT LIKE TO LIVE IN MIAMI?	20

FAKE PLASTIC TREES	22
TOO DARK (PART I)	23

II.

WINTER	27
NEW YEAR'S EVE	28
NEW YEAR'S DAY	29
WHAT'S YOUR SPIRIT ANIMAL?	30
THE VELVET ROOM	31
VIOLET	32
LOVE POEM FOR PERIMENOPAUSAL WOMEN	33
NIGHT WATCH	34
DOING IT DOLLY STYLE	35
CLOUD ON MY TONGUE	36
TOO DARK (PART II)	37
DEAR SYLVIA:	38
DEAR GIANNI:	39
DEAR BETTY:	40
DEAR MOTHER:	41
SUNDAYS ARE FOR ELEGIES	42
THE FUTURE	43

III.

SPRING	47
HOMETEL	48
PUBLIC TRANSIT	49
DEAD CAT	50
I CAN'T SEE MIAMI	51
A FLAMBOYANCE OF FLAMINGOS	52
CENTO FOR 17 MUTUALS	53
NOT CLEAR	54

IV.

SUMMER	57
IT'S ALWAYS SUMMER IN MIAMI	58
FIND ME	59
TACO BELL IS $\geq$ THERAPY	60
FATHER PAUL, I…	61
'80s RAUNCH	62
FAST FOOD COUNTER	63
PAY THE POETS!	64
LOVE POEM FOR DR. MELFI	65

THE MOON IS GAY (AKA SAY GAY!)	66
LOVE POEM FOR FIRE-STAR	67
BLANK SPACE	68
THE MARIJUANA STATE	69
GARGOYLES AND GROTESQUES	70
FRENCH EDUCATION	71
DEAR LANA:	72
DEAR TOPPS COMPANY:	73
AURORA STARR SAYS…	75
RED TIDE	76
CITY OF HOPE	77

EPILOGUE

(SHORT) LOVE POEM FOR MIAMI	81
(LONG) LOVE POEM FOR MIAMI	82
VERSACE	92

For Miami, Michigan, Militza, Mom, & Maureen

PROLOGUE

FERSACE

I moved to Miami because of The Golden Girls and The Conga. True story. Versace and a job offer may have played a small role. I took a government job, so I'm wearing FERSACE. That's not a typo. I can't afford the real VERSACE. At least not in suit form. Forgive me, Gianni.

So much here is plastic. It's almost impossible for nature to stand out. No, I didn't move here for the weather. That was actually a deterrent. I spent the first year in the AC anyway. I miss the four seasons.

I miss my mother. She died six years ago. Ovarian cancer. It was awful. What cancer isn't? Maybe the astrological sign. I should know. I am one. I don't think I'm awful. You can ask my partner. (Yes, I'm gay.) She's a Pisces. She may be biased because her moon is in Cancer though.

POEM FOR PARIS HILTON

Paris Hilton is a better poet than I am.
She says *That's hot*™ & *Sliving*™ & people listen.
Everyone repeat after Paris: I'm *sliving*™.
If you aren't watching Cooking With Paris,
you aren't *sliving*™.
Paris says *sliving*™ is the new *That's hot.*™
Paris says "It's slaying & living your best life in one word."
Paris is a genius.
(Don't be jealous.)
If you're a poet & you aren't watching Cooking With Paris, you should be.
Paris is coining language with every episode.
"Cotton candy is just sugar with more personality."
She said that during my favorite episode: "Taco Night With Saweetie."
Paris & Saweetie cooking shrimp tacos in couture?
That's *sliving*™.
She also said, "News flash: Truffle oil is rich bitch shit."
And then she said, "Saweetie should totally trademark that."
Yes, Saweetie should.
Before Paris does.
Loves it.™
The Oxford Dictionary of Quotes takes Paris' words seriously.
So does Dictionary.com.
Look it up.
Are words you invented in any dictionary?
I didn't think so.
I invented a word.
It's FERSACE.
I'm trademarking it right here.
FERSACE™.
It's the word for fake (or faux, if you're French or fancy) VERSACE products.
I see a lot of FERSACE™ in Miami.
Maybe Paris will read this poem & say *FERSACE*™ during the next season of Cooking With Paris.

(There will be a season 2 someday…right, Netflix?!)
"Kim, what do you think about those poor people in Miami who can only afford FERSACE™?"
"It's so sad. They aren't *sliving*™."
Bam! FERSACE™ goes viral.
FERSACE™ gets added to Dictionary.com.
Maybe I'll get some royalties for my creative capital & can buy some real VERSACE.
Maybe people will listen to my words.
Maybe I'll be as good a poet as Paris Hilton is.

NOT SEEN

Who are you?	YOURSELF
What is your name?	NOT SEEN
Are you a good spirit?	YES
When will it snow again?	SUMMER
Does it snow in the summer where you are?	YES
Is the snow cold?	NO
Where are you?	FAR AWAY
Is there time where you are?	2 TIMES
What does that mean?	CANNOT SAY
Why not?	UNSAFE
Are you afraid?	NO
Should I be afraid?	MAYBE LATER
Are you in Heaven or Hell?	HELL
Is Hell cold?	YES
Is it winter?	NO
What season is it?	FALL

I.

FALL

Fall—died on January 3, 2006, when I officially moved to Florida. Fall was my mother's favorite season before she died. I think it was probably mine, too. But I'm no longer sure what I love.

Do I just love everything that my mother did? The leaves falling from trees turning blue.

They say blue is the warmest color, but I say it's orange. My mother painted so many stills of trees. She said her favorite color was red, but she painted all the leaves bright orange. I never asked her why. I was too self-absorbed to ask her much of anything.

When my friend L mailed me two of my dead mother's paintings, I cried for days. All the bright orange I remembered had faded to brown. My mother hated brown. I fingered the canvases of our past for clues. They told me to look inside.

RIFLE SEASON

Where I come from, there's a season for guns, as if rifles should be celebrated like Christmas.

There's a smell. I'd like to call it November, but it's a special blend of blood, rust, estrus, and a fall so cold it freezes the hair inside my nose.

There's a ritual. It's men dressed in camouflage and hunter orange. It's the law. And they stay out late on the 40 and chug 40s, perch up in trees or shelter in blinds, chew tobacco and build big fires.

Where I come from, it's also about the merchandise. The "Nice Rack" shirts and mounted deer heads on the wall. Not surprisingly, racks are one reason men prize the buck more than the doe.

There's a sound out my window where I come from. It's earsplitting gunfire and the fight between my uncle and cousin who I thought would never speak again.

There's a name for the soft boys where I come from, the ones who don't drive big trucks and don't refer to women as broads you just load up and throw in the back.

Where I come from, hunting is a blood sport. And it breeds blood-thirsty boys who think it's ok to say: Do what I say or I'll shoot you.

There's also a mascot: a dead deer, purple gray tongue out, gutted and hanging from the rafters of the garage. The same purple gray of the deer liver my dad left on the counter for my mom to cook.

She said it reminded her of afterbirth and made her gag.

DYING YOUNG

I grew up in the middle of a cornfield, went to college in the middle of a cornfield. The smell of manure would wake me some mornings. I can remember my grandfather tossing me like a sack of old potatoes into the corn grinder for fun. I remember thinking I would lose a limb or two, before being ground to cornmeal. I remember cleaning the horse stables. Gagging in the hay. I remember picking sweet and sour berries, thorns tearing at my tender fingers. And later picking seeds out of my teeth after eating too many blackberries. The sun so hot shining down. I can still smell the dust and dirt—the change in the air and the rain from summer to fall. I remember fall in the haunted cornfield. Flannel. Black nails. Ghost stories. Reapers. Mazes. Hunts for crop circles and witches. Reading a Book of Shadows. Playing Light as a Feather, Stiff as a Board. Us heathens, summoning Candyman and Bloody Mary, in and out of mirrors. Taking swigs from a shared bottle of Boone's Farm. A fire, always a big fire, to soften the October blow. Someone telling a story of someone who died young among the corn. Who told the story, and who died young—that, that I can't remember.

THE HOLY TRINITY

I went through a phase post college when I dressed like Trinity from *The Matrix*. It lasted two years and would have lasted longer had professional obligations not demanded I drop the black boots and vinyl trench. I'm recalling a conversation now in which the president of the company where I worked in PR had his son pull me aside and ask me what was up with my nose ring.

It was a very small diamond stud that I did not have when they hired me. *You are the face of this company*, he said. And my thought was, *Exactly*. Maybe we all shouldn't look like the same version of the tired Midwest soccer mom with the bad highlights who bakes you too-sweet brownies for your birthday. I didn't say that.

I don't remember what I said, but I didn't remove it, and they kept me anyway. Because I was good at getting cover stories and the design editors in New York liked me. It was probably because of my all-black attire, but I digress.

I did end up leaving to go to another company where that president drank a $700 bottle of wine, called 9-1-1, and later shot himself in the head the day before Thanksgiving. Some might say that job wasn't a good career move for me. But I ended up getting a really good job after that.

DEAR LORDE:

I want you to know that I've been known to listen to "Royals" on repeat for several hours at a time. It's one of my go-to mood lifters when I'm having a bad day. It's also one of the few songs on the radio I will argue is never overplayed. And that's a compliment coming from me because I'm generally annoyed by repetitive sounds.

Speaking of mood, I also want you to know that I kind of like the lyrics to "Mood Ring." I honestly hadn't heard the *Solar Power* album until someone half my age told me I should listen to it. Good thing I have younger friends and Apple Music because I probably would have missed out otherwise.

It could be because I'm a Cancer, but "Mood Ring" feels like it was written just for me. I know you're a water sign, too, so you get it. I also know I'm probably not a member of your target audience because I likely won't venture much beyond listening to "Royals" on repeat, but I sincerely want to thank you for writing a song that's taken me to my happy place since 2013.

MAMI

In Michigan, they
called me *kid*. In Miami,
they call me *mami*.

A WOMAN CALLED MY FACE

older than what she expected.
A plastic woman I didn't know in Palm Beach
who had seen it first in a photo
online, and then in person when I showed up
to a party she invited me to based solely on what
she thought was my youth. I thought
for a moment to apologize, but I stopped myself
because why should I say I'm sorry for what I've earned
with time?

DEAR BARBIE:

Tell me all your secrets. You never age or gain weight. A little nip and tuck over the years perhaps? Well, you look fantastic. Now if we're telling secrets, I'll tell you one: I never much liked you, but pretended to be a fan to please my friend A.

Tell me, what do you think of the real-life Barbie who sustains herself on air? Or all the girls who starve themselves to live up your impossible beauty standards? I know it's not entirely your fault. You didn't ask to be born so freakishly disproportionate, or to never age.

Here's a thought: What if you convince your handlers to let you show some wrinkles? Even your 96-year-old-Iris Apfel iteration is wrinkle-free. How about a BOTOX-free debut? You could do some real good by letting the real you come out and play.

Come on, Doll. What do you say?

Sincerely,

Aging naturally in Miami

FLACA

In Michigan, they
called me *broad*. In Miami,
they call me *flaca*.

HEMINGWAY DRANK MOJITOS AND OTHER MIAMI MYTHS

Everyone is Cuban.
Everyone does cocaine.
Everyone is at the club 24/7.
Everyone owns a $100,000 car.
Everyone lives in South Beach.
No one speaks English.
The weather is always gorgeous.
It's always Spring Break in Miami

GRINGA

In Michigan, they
called me *dyke*. In Miami,
they call me *gringa*.

WHAT'S IT LIKE TO LIVE IN MIAMI?

It's too much and not enough, depending on the day. It's like living anywhere new. So seductive at first and then the sheen slowly peels away. Except here, there is sun. So much sun. Do you love the sun?

Then you will love it here. But what do you really want me to tell you? That living here will be easier? It won't. After a while, everyone gets sick of the sun. And wherever you go, you find yourself again.

Your brand-new suit will get old, and you can't ever lose yourself in it for long. The new trees will become old trees, and the new birds will become old birds, and what seduced you will soon wrinkle and bruise and fade to the ugliest brown.

It's joy, constant joy. It's a sunshine state of mind. It's what Will Smith sings about, and Nicki Minaj too. It's hot pink, it's bright blue, it's neon orange. It's the '80s in the '20s. The 2020s. It's the past, present and future.

It's summer on the happiest day of your youth. It's the best breakfast you've ever had, enjoyed in the company of your closest friends. It's a burst of shameless laughter. It's the best birthday you can remember. It's the rainbow over the sky after days of rain. After the downpour and the deluge.

It's the warmest hug. It doesn't let go first. It keeps on holding on to you. It asks: *Are you ok?* Even though it already knows the answer. Of course you're ok. You live in someone's fantasy, someone's paradise.

FAKE PLASTIC TREES

The grass isn't always greener except when it is. I'm reporting live from where the grass is legit greener. And it is *really* green. Too green. That fake grass is always going to be greener than the real thing. But that doesn't make it any better.

No one warned me that when I got palms, I'd eventually want pines, and when I got those pines, I'd miss the palms. How the cold can comfort more than the heat—until it reaches extremes. And yes, it can be too hot here, too cold there, and too green anywhere.

Trees can be implants too.
Did you know that?
Do you know where it is just enough green?

TOO DARK (PART I)

Who are you?	ONE FROM YOUR PAST
What is your name?	TOO DARK
Are you a good spirit?	NO
Do you want to harm me?	NO
What do you want me to know?	UNCLEAR
What is my purpose in this life?	FUTURE HAZY
Are you ok?	NO
Can I help?	NO
Can I speak to Sylvia Plath?	NO
Can I speak to Gianni Versace?	NO
Can I speak to Betty White?	NO
Can I speak to my mother?	YES
How do I talk to her?	ASK
When will I die?	WINTER
How will I die?	LEAVE ME NOW

II.

WINTER

It's the coldest day of the year in most of the world, but I'm still sweating in the summer sun. There is no white snow here, only sand. Christmas hits different with lights strung around palm trees instead of pines. Relatives send photos of snowbanks blocking front doors and burying cars.

I move about without layers or falling. There is no wool to warm or ice to melt. People sell hot chocolate anyway, with a side of cinnamon churros. I light a candle that smells like winter wood burning. I call that smell *home*.

I once saw an iguana fall from a tree when the temperature dropped to 50. I wish it were 50 today. No, I wish it were 30. I wish the sky would open again like it did the year after I was born. We would feel the snow freeze our eyelashes.

We would live a real Christmas miracle. *Sweet Baby Jesus*, we'd say. Angels dropping white frozen feathers down on Florida from above. Little cold kisses from the winter gods, covering our sunscreened faces.

NEW YEAR'S EVE

Too much champagne and food again. I'm avoiding people and parties, and the smell of meat and resolve. A fire in Miami. It's heat too hot. I turn on the TV to *Law & Order SVU*. Looking for hope in consistency. A cup of Nespresso.

Is this what each new year will look like going forward? We can no longer entertain ourselves. So many screens. Nothing feels new. My jaw that pops and the fear of everything decrepit. Kiss my partner. Joke that she's stuck with me.

I remember the high of new boots and short dresses. The snow brushing my bare shoulders, waiting in line at the latest club. Faux fur coat that I didn't want to check. Sticky dance floor. Too much champagne, a shower of it. The droplets freezing to my skin on the long walk home alone.

NEW YEAR'S DAY

A new year and the same old season.
A broken record playing the same sad song.
It seems ungrateful to be sick of summer.
It seems like heaven to have year-round sun.
This is why I think hell is hot—I've lived it.
My mother believed hell was ice cold.
She was always worried about me freezing.
She thought she would winter in Miami.
She thought we would enjoy long walks in the sun.
I walk outside alone now, long after the sun has gone down.
I have lost more than just the four seasons.
I have lost the leaves and the snow.
I have lost my most reliable cache clock.
I have lost my home and my soul.

WHAT'S YOUR SPIRIT ANIMAL?

The one you really relate to, not the one you tell people when asked in a professional setting. Like the time I told an interviewer I was a cheetah because I'm fast (sort of) and resourceful (definitely), when I really wanted to say I'm a snowy owl because I like to appear when I want to.

And limit human interaction. And I like the winter. But that's not something you say in an interview in Miami. I mean, unless you don't want the job. And I did want it (at the time) and did get it, in case you're wondering.

Well, the snowy owl is my true spirit animal, and I'm saying it now and going forward. I could be happy alone for hours, or just chilling as the mascot for some library, or hanging out with Harry Potter and all the other introverts who really just want to remain magically mysterious.

What's your spirit animal? That's not a rhetorical question. I'm trying to find my fellow snowy owls or maybe the grizzly bears who like to hibernate in the winter. You can DM me @natallman, if Twitter's still around.

THE VELVET ROOM

In fifth grade, I carried a grape
Scratch 'n Sniff Sticker in my pants pocket
wherever I went.

I also carried a copy of a heavy,
faded book the school librarian
reserved especially for me.

Mrs. Woodward reminded me
of a mouse being chased
by an owl.

Someone said something
about her living
with another woman.

We weren't supposed
to speak of it,
although no one ever told me that directly.

My sticker
became my bookmark.
By winter, my book smelled like an old vineyard.

Even now, if I close my eyes,
the curtained room
velvets and purples.

VIOLET

A winter wish for the taste
of snow in my mouth—
pill or real, does it matter?

The way the grey stills us all.
I have been blue in my tired for so long.
Iris, let my rest come to me—

deep and violet.
No, it doesn't matter.
Let it come in fragments.

Let it come.
Angels dust my eyes with feathers
from their white, white, wings.

They aren't ready for me there yet.
There's so much left here
we haven't even seen.

LOVE POEM FOR PERIMENOPAUSAL WOMEN

I'm like a birch tree in the naked white of winter.
The birch that autocorrect first changed to *bitch* then *butch*.

I'm shedding layers of black and white paper and ash.
Newspapers have never been more alive or dead,

as I silence my phone and turn to
phonographs, still photography, and vinyl.

Here I find comfort,
among the old, the dusty, the musty, and familiar—the 1880s

and the 1980s
the granny panties and overwhelming old French perfumes.

Here I crank up the heady rose,
the saccharine violet, the languid linden blossom,

resurrect the pink fluorescent
of my faded Electric Youth.

NIGHT WATCH

The stars in the sky wear watches tonight. They count time more slowly than I—or is it me? I could look it up, but I don't care about grammar today. I care that I count everything quickly. The yellow of the day and the black of the night.

My psychiatrist taught me the word *nyctophilia*. Yes, I like the dark more than the light. The way my anxiety shrinks with the sunset. The calm that comes when everyone else is asleep.

Have you ever lived in town small enough to go silent at 10 p.m., or one that closed down for the snow? Some of my closest friends need sun lamps to cope with the Michigan gray. I coped by moving to Miami and now suffer the sunny winter.

Well-meaning people tell me to go out more in the sun. I tell them I only like the beach when it's overcast. I tell them paradise is relative. I tell them I'm happiest in the moonlight. They tell me I'm just depressed. I tell them maybe. I tell them I've tried all the pills. I tell them to let me enjoy the dark.

DOING IT DOLLY STYLE

One winter, I went to Tennessee, but skipped out on Dollywood. I tend to avoid doing what I'm told I must do. Like working a 9 to 5 job, having kids, and marrying a man. No thank you. What's the appeal in doing what everyone says we should?

When a well-meaning local said, *You can't come to Pigeon Forge without seeing Dollywood*, I high tailed it straight to Memphis. Cranked "Jolene" the whole drive there. I think Dolly would approve. And when I got to Memphis, I skipped out on Graceland too.

CLOUD ON MY TONGUE

All the girls here are freezing cold
Stripped of their most bewitching powers
They shiver like swans in March's hold

Another empty day in this empty city of gold
No one waters the winter flowers
All the girls here are freezing cold

All the girls here are a hundred years old
Now masters of the touchless hours
They quiver like swans in March's hold

The jealous frost rains down a raging white cold
Blasting the wrath of the cooling towers
All the girls here have seized the cold

All the lady petals refuse to fold
A strong flower never long cowers
It blooms bigger in March's fiercest hold

All the winter roses have grown so bold
A self-watered flower never sours
All the girls here have seized the cold
They shimmer like swans in March's hold

TOO DARK (PART II)

TOO DARK says I can speak to some of the dead if I ask. I ask if he's a good spirit or bad. He says he's bad. I once heard the loud flutter of black wings, opened my eyes, and saw you floating above my bed. In stage one of the bardo passage, lamas attending to the deceased urge them to accept that they are dead. Every time the dead appear without me calling, I say, *You are dead. You are dead. You are dead.*

DEAR SYLVIA:

TOO DARK told me I couldn't speak to you through my Ouija board, so I'm going to try to reach you through this poem. I want you to know how famous you are now and how many people adore you. My favorite poem of yours is "Tulips" and I also really love "Edge," which is credited as the last known poem you wrote, but that's debatable because Ted burned your last journal. That's also debatable.

I also want you to know that there's a 1,154-page biography about you called *Red Comet* and that your tarot deck recently sold on Sotheby's for $200,000. Can you believe that? Can you believe that some of your fans take a trip to Indiana just to see your braid? Others go to your grave in Heptonstall to deface the Hughes name from your headstone.

You also have a bot that is quite active on Twitter. You probably don't know what that means, but I think you may have liked Twitter and would have had a lot of followers. Ok, you probably wouldn't have liked Twitter, but you definitely would have had a lot of followers. I would have loved to follow you.

I follow Frieda for you on Instagram. You probably don't know what that means either, but it's a place where she posts photos of a menagerie of pets (including 14 owls!), paintings, cooking, nature walks, motorbikes, and flowers. I learned from Instagram that she had a big art exhibit in London recently.

Frieda looks a lot like you. She has also published several children's books and several poetry books. I want you to know that she seems to be doing well—in spite of it all. She still has your laundry box seat from the 1950s. She says she painted her feelings onto it.

DEAR GIANNI:

For my birthday in 2020, I booked a room at Casa Casuarina to celebrate not being dead. I swam in your pool at night after everyone went to bed. I also ran up to the observatory to see if I could reach you through the red. You didn't take my call, so I left you a heady trail of roses there instead.

DEAR BETTY:

I once watched a TV interview in which you said that your mother had a great relationship to death. You explained that she believed we can rejoice in the dead because they finally know the secret to what happens after we die. Now that you know, tell me: Where do we go, Betty?

You can try reach me through TOO DARK, or maybe my cat. Like Constantine says: They're "half in, half out anyway." You were able to break through barriers here. I think you can break through there.

I don't know where there is, but not too long ago, I received a copy of *People* magazine in the mail with you on the cover. It ceremoniously proclaimed: "Betty White Turns 100!" You didn't quite make it to 100, but the joke's on them. You made the cover anyway.

DEAR MOTHER:

There are three sounds I can't forget—
    death rattle
        last breath
            the zap of energy from one plane to the next.

I would like to write a poem in which you appear
    to me in a dream,
        and then,
            I would like to
                ask you several questions:

Where did you go after your heart   stopped at 4:44 p.m.?
Did you finally   get your wings?
Are you an angel, a bird,   another creature I have yet to see?
Would you come back if you could?   Why haven't you?
Why don't you answer when   I call your name?

        MOTHER,
            WHERE
                HAVE
                    YOU
                        GONE?

    TOO DARK says I can speak to you if I just ask.

        MOTHER,
            CAN
                YOU
                    HEAR
                      ME?

Mors tē numquam sistat.   Mors tē numquam sistat.   Mors tē numquam sistat.
Mors tē numquam sistat.   Mors tē numquam sistat.   Mors tē numquam sistat.

SUNDAYS ARE FOR ELEGIES

and by that, I mean: Let the rain out. I've got enough sadness for 7 more blood moons. Flutter to the ground like the wing-cut fly stunned mid-flight. Stay down for a while. Stay still. Drink only rose water. Maybe a little thyme. Going to write your name until the ink runs out of blue. Until the day runs dry.

THE FUTURE

Who are you?	ONE TO BE FEARED
What is your name?	THE FUTURE
Are you a good spirit?	YES
Will I be happy in Miami?	NO
Should I move back to Michigan?	NO
Where should I move?	CLOSE
Where is close?	AT A CROSSROADS
What season is it where you are?	TOO HOT
Is it summer?	NO
Is it winter?	NO
Is it spring?	UNKNOWN

III.

SPRING

They say there are two seasons in Michigan, winter and construction. But today it feels like spring. I'm getting comfortable again with feeling. Must all the poets fully feel our senses? I was pretty comfortable feeling numb. I was pretty comfortable being dead to the four seasons. It's surprisingly easy to be sad when it's always summer.

And then comes the hurricane rain—that muddy welcome-mat intrusion. That smell of the languid lake, and the birds trilling louder as we speak of the dead. They want to join us. Who is the "they" in this poem? Is it the living or the dead? By living do I mean the virgin maples in the forest, or the deceased ceilings made of knotty pine?

I think they both can hear us. I hear the orchids could bloom here under the right conditions. But we keep cutting everything that grows differently right down. Spring is different when there's no snow before it. When the crocuses have nothing hard to push through. When the bitter winter never comes.

HOMETEL

That spring when R asked if I lived in a hometel, and I almost corrected him but stopped myself because I realized small children sometimes understand truths better than adults do, and that their vocabulary is consequently at times far superior.

It's irrelevant that I lived in a residential high-rise and not a hotel. It's relevant that this friend's child equated elevator with hotel. Doorman with hotel. No backyard with hotel. Not quite a home is a hometel. What do you think makes a home a home?

PUBLIC TRANSIT

I tumbled down two entire flights of stairs while exiting a Metromover station one spring and no one offered to help me up. Before boarding the train today, however, the automated announcer warns me to stand back from the platform. On the train, I must stay clear of the doors, she says. Not because she cares, but because departure is being delayed. For my safety, she tells me to hold the handrails. That doesn't feel safe these days, and the hand-sanitizer dispenser is empty. A sign says if I feel unsafe onboard, I can call 375-2700. Who can I call if I feel unsafe once I exit?

DEAD CAT

One Spring Break, while sipping frozen margaritas and lounging on flamingo floats in a friend's pool, my friend K told me the story of how she keeps her dead cat in the freezer next to her mother's dead puppy. She stores him in a garbage bag between a jumbo bag of pot-stickers and margarita mix. The cat is black, in case you're wondering. I know because I asked. I also asked why she didn't bury them both in the backyard. She said she said there simply wasn't space. The cat died young. She suspected it was parvo contracted from her mother's new puppy. I had to Google parvo, which I learned is short for parvovirus—a highly contagious disease often spread by direct contact with infected blood, feces, urine or other bodily fluids. I didn't ask the cat's name. I should have. Would it be weird to bring it up again now? Should I just text her: What's the name of the dead cat you keep in the freezer? I guess I could. I mean, she did seem ok talking about it. I think enough time has passed. She also told me how her estranged father was semi-famous for suing a police officer for stealing his severed leg. Then she told me how she can't seem to keep a boyfriend or a girlfriend for long, which is surprising because she has a lot of great stories.

I CAN'T SEE MIAMI

from Michigan, but I can see what has changed me. I can't walk in the woods without anxiety. I say: *Where is the 24/7 CVS and the lavender chai latte?* I say, *I'm so cold.* D says, *You think you're a big shot now*, wants to slap it out of me.

They say the apple doesn't fall far from the tree, but I'm falling as far away as possible. Got lots of therapy. I know Miami isn't home, but what is home? I can't seem to find it. I know it's not the bottom of a wine glass or a cheating girlfriend. It's not a big bank account or a high-profile career.

My yoga teacher says, *Be in the moment*, but I don't know how. Don't you feel time racing? Don't you see everyone around us dying? I think I'm here to write 33 books, but I've only written three. I ask the Universe to guide me. A coconut falls like thunder from a palm.

A FLAMBOYANCE OF FLAMINGOS

There are no flamingos on Lake Michigan, which may be why it took me moving to Miami to figure out that a group of them is called a flamboyance. Maybe I'm not as smart as I think I am. Or as smart as other people think I am. Like my friend G, who called me "learned" when he learned that I spoke French fluently. And I thought I wasn't all that special, but I guess to him I was because I spoke more than just English. He said he wasn't used to white people trying. Exposure. Yes, I was exposed. I learned through osmosis. Was it that summer in Aix, or that winter in Montreal? That time I spent chasing around married French women, learning I'm not all that smart after all.

CENTO FOR 17 MUTUALS

I swallowed a pill; I swallowed a pine cone.
The world ends like an almond tree pulled by its roots.
I don't want to drive my car into that tree anymore.

Cold spot near mom's favorite recliner,
I've nothing to offer but
that deer there, cracked at the spine, oozing onto roadside
rock.

My days are numbered, just like yours.
I flinch at each number like a gun has gone off.
I'll be dead soon enough—

cradled above the earth, rocked gently to sleep
to a primal white sky, wheeling on.
I worried there'd be nothing more than a silver vortex.

In places like this, I am a ghost,
a serpent that rattles against silent stone floors,
in a room with glimpses of yesterday, displayed along alabaster
walls.

Once I watched a boy disappear under the surface a lake.
Some words are too big to mean anything.
I'm saving the story for the afterlife.

There's no need to close the door on your way out.

NOT CLEAR

Who are you?	NO ONE
What is your name?	NOT CLEAR
Are you a good spirit?	YES
Where are you?	A FAMILIAR PLACE
Can you be more specific?	NORTH
Are you in Heaven?	NO
Are you in Hell?	YES
Hell is north?	YES
Is it hot?	NO
How did you get there?	UNKNOWN
Where were you before this?	FAR AWAY
Where are you going next?	A DARK PLACE
What's it called?	SUMMER

IV.

SUMMER

is eating a whole bag of Twizzlers by yourself or an entire box of Otter Pops, save the Poncho Punch because I don't like fruit punch, even less so after I witnessed a friend vomit an entire jug of Hawaiian Punch onto the seat of a Ferris wheel in high school.

Do you remember when National Pax tried to replace Sir Isaac Lime with Scarlett O'Cherry and a Stanford professor accused the company of otter-cide? I don't either, but I remember reading about it later.

What is your favorite summer memory and why is it tied to food? (Proust might have a clue.) Is it a picnic or a BBQ? Is it paddleboating around a lake sharing a box of NERDS? Is it eating too many s'mores or hotdogs by a bonfire?

My grandma used to make me a lemon pineapple cake with whipped cream frosting every year for my birthday in July. She worked in a bakery after my grandpa died. It never really feels like summer, or my birthday, without that cake, but I still try.

When did summer die for you?

IT'S ALWAYS SUMMER IN MIAMI

It's always summer
in Miami. The heat hell-
ish and heavenly.

FIND ME

Find me on Miami Beach, wearing a track suit instead of a bathing suit.

Find me hiding under an umbrella.

Find me ignoring the sound of your Reggaeton.

Find me turning down your invitation to party.

Find me unable to ignore the scrape of the sand between my toes.

Find me uncomfortably sticky with excess sunscreen.

Find me wearing sunglasses, even when it's cloudy.

(They'll be real VERSACE. I spend good money avoiding eye contact.)

Find me avoiding eye contact.

Find me enjoying the last of the champagne.

Find me loving the dark.

TACO BELL IS ≥ THERAPY

One summer, I paid Taco Bell more than my therapist, and that is saying a lot. My therapist said to get up and do something when I couldn't sleep. Ever live in a town so small that every sit-down restaurant closes at 10 p.m.? Ever get anxiety and go to Taco Bell just to have a stranger take your order at 3 a.m.? Ever cry at a Taco Bell drive-thru when asked: *How are you doing tonight, Sweetheart?* Ever wish Taco Bell sold alcohol? Ever wish you could live a little less? Ever drown your sorrows in a Spicy Bean Burrito? Ever buy that promotional plush Chihuahua you really didn't need? Ever have your mother ask why you have so many unused packets of mild sauce in your cabinet? Ever have your therapist proudly tell you her son could eat a whole six-pack of tacos by himself? Ever wonder how that was relevant to the depression you were telling her about? Ever never see that therapist again? Ever wean yourself off Effexor and go to Taco Bell instead?

FATHER PAUL, I...

grew up without a church, borrowed a pew at a friend's in the summer. Drank the cloying fruit punch they served out of too-small paper cups. Ate their off-brand cookies. It was often dark and cool—the only light coming through the stained-glass windows. Light fractured like a prism. I stood at the feet of the crucified Jesus. Felt the puncture of nails and thorns. Put the dollar my mother gave me in the gold offering bowl. Everyone always seemed sad and solemn. I don't remember joy, but restraint. The smell of wax and bleach. The organ droning on. The few people who weren't tone deaf leading the chorus. My mind always wandering somewhere, anywhere, but there. To running outside in the grass. To playing Monkey in the Middle. To coloring. To Lazarus. To Gabriel. To Mary. To sin and suffering. To blood. To the priest in his simple robes. To the little green Bible he gave me. To his unwavering belief that he could actually save me. To the girls I wanted to hug a little too long.

'80s RAUNCH

The movies I watched at night as a kid in the '80s were mostly raunchy. They were also mostly watched in basements. During summer slumber parties at a friend's house where we also played Truth or Dare and Girl Talk.

Movies were meant to quiet us down after we practiced hand-over-mouth kissing and gave each other makeovers. We'd somehow manage to find the movies we shouldn't be watching. No one stopped us.

We watched *Spaceballs*, *Porky's*, and all the Molly Ringwald movies. I was obsessed with *Sixteen Candles*. I related to flat-chested Samantha and crushed on Caroline. And though it was rated PG, it had all the good makings of a hot '80s teen movie: nudity, swearing, sex, fast cars, a school dance.

And yes, I know *Sixteen Candles* hasn't aged well—with its racism and rape culture. At 10, I didn't have the tools to register this. I just thought it was sad that Samantha's family forgot her birthday. I thought that would never happen to me, until I came out at 22 and my family conveniently forgot mine.

FAST FOOD COUNTER

I worked at McDonald's one summer in high school, but only because my mother made me. The manager looked me up and down on day one and said, *No back kitchen for you. You're too pretty.* Sent me straight to the front counter. I should have quit on the spot, but I didn't.

Put on a purple shirt the color of Grimace and an ugly matching visor. Sold those burgers and super-size fries to even creepier guys than him. Burned my arm badly on the fry cooker and went home smelling like salt and grease.

Worked with a guy who rode his bicycle to and from work in a blizzard. He defended me when the customers got too aggressive over not having enough mustard or pickles. He also took the food the manager said to throw away home every night to his kids. Said we were blessed to have a job.

PAY THE POETS!

Pay the poets!
In real money, not just in flowers or free drinks or books!

Give us rock star status!
World tour all the poets (not just Rupi) in the fancy concert halls!

Dress us up in ball gowns or tuxes and in VERSACE or Chanel!
Some poets may not like this fanfare, being shy or introverted or both.

But you can still pay the poets!
Some rock stars are shy and introverted, and you pay them beaucoup.

So, pay the poets!
We're writing lyrics and performing on stages just for you.

Who said not to pay the poets?
We like nice things—trips, wine and perfume.

And having the necessities, like housing, healthcare and food.
We're working all kinds of crazy jobs just to pay our bills.

Please pay the poets, so we don't have to work at [insert name of non-poetry workplace here]!
We're writing these poems for posterity, often for free and always for you.

LOVE POEM FOR DR. MELFI

I was 22 when I first saw *The Sopranos*—around the same summer I came out to my parents and started talking about my true attractions with my friends. I've always liked smart, older women. Even better when they're confident and authoritative—like Olivia Benson in *Law & Order: SVU*, and Dr. Melfi on *The Sopranos*.

Sure, Adriana is conventionally hotter, with that blonde hair and those vampy outfits. She also checks my age-appropriateness box a little bit better. But what does age matter when it's fantasy anyway? It's not like any of these characters and I will ever be together. And, yeah, there's the psychological factor to bear in mind too when we consider the root of our attractions.

I was once compared to Proust by an older woman who happened to be my professor. She said I had mommy issues, which I later discovered is quite typical of Cancers. And it may or may not be noteworthy that the actress who plays Dr. Melfi is a Libra whose birthday is the day before my mother's.

But you can't tell me Dr. Melfi doesn't have a certain something special. That surface rigidity. That added challenge. That tough love. That stability. That togetherness. That I'm here for you 24/7. That prescription pad. That confidence. That I know you better than you know yourself. That abrupt exit. That unfulfilled desire. That attractive abandonment.

THE MOON IS GAY (AKA SAY GAY!)

It's June and the moon is looking even gayer tonight. She's in Gemini—shining her super social waxing crescent moon face. I was born under a crescent moon. Yes, I was also born gay. That really isn't debatable.

There is no rainbow moon, but there should be. Rainbow Brite would live there, along with her best Twink-friend sprite. They would wake every night, singing: *Sunbeams sparkle and shine/ You'll always be a friend of mine*. '80s gay kids will remember that theme-song line.

When I told my mother I was gay, she said, *But you were a cheerleader!* I love that gay movie with Natasha Lyonne. Have you seen it? Watch it tonight, if you haven't. And then go outside and enjoy the gay moon. Or wait until the next full moon. Maybe you'll catch a gay moonbow.

LOVE POEM FOR FIRE-STAR

Name a heroine hotter than Fire-Star. I don't think you can. I've been crushing on her since she debuted in summer 1981. Yes, I was only 5, but I knew fire then. I was glued to the TV. I had a thing for redheads. And she is magma. She is lava. No, she's the whole damn volcano. With a single glance, she set me on fire. That red hair against yellow costume fire. She's a red comet soaring high above the moon. She's radioactive. She's microwave radiation manipulation. She's full-on flight. She's energy wavelength disruption. She's the zap that kills the microwave in the night. She's a trained assassin. She's loyal. She's single. She's probably still in love with Iceman.

BLANK SPACE

I once listened to "Blank Space" on repeat for eight straight hours while making my way from Miami to Michigan in the midst of a bad summer breakup. I didn't absorb much of the lyrics, but something about the idea of love as torture bore singing, sobbing and repeating.

I do love the occasional earworm. I also love the use of f-word alliteration: forever, flames, friends, and getting swept up in a Taylor tide of rapidly shifting emotions. The fact that people who have strong feelings are called crazy or otherwise shamed for expressing them is shameful.

Someone once said Taylor Swift was the modern Sylvia—mostly for "Look What You Made Me Do." Didn't quite buy it at the time. Argued that Tori was my jam, but Taylor can leave you pretty bloody too.

THE MARIJUANA STATE

A McDonald's highway sign says: Choose your chill, Michigan
But I don't think Netflix is on the menu.

When did this state turn into a giant marijuana ad?
I remember when Michigan humbly peddled furniture.

I can no longer come here without mourning my mother.
To look at a lake is to see her pink shadow.

People in Miami don't get me when I show them my right hand.
I point at it and say: "This is where I'm from."

They ask: Isn't that where you can't drink the water?
I say: Maybe, but we're The Great Lakes State.

They ask: Isn't that where you get a free gun when you open a bank account?
I say: Maybe, but I was never offered one.

I say: I don't know what else to say.
Maybe I'll just say we're The Marijuana State from now on.

GARGOYLES AND GROTESQUES

The old buildings I love most are occupied by gargoyles and grotesques. Half-human, half-animal. The more terrifying, the better. I feel guarded by what terrifies others. The horned one at the top of Notre Dame is my favorite. Gemory. That hideous beast. He would tear the heart right out of a lecherous man's chest and eat it for a midnight snack.

I once had a whole camera roll full of photos of the gargoyles who guarded me from the lecherous men in my path. The word *gargoyle* in French, *gargouille*, comes from the Latin word for throat. I like throaty words like the French like their cigarettes—how they can be swallowed in slow, long, drags.

My friend C used to imitate the faces of grotesques when we would walk the cobbled summer streets of France. She would hiss, all spittle and throaty, as if she were being strangled to her death. *Do I scare you?* she would ask, eyes bulging maniacally from their sockets. I would tell her *yes*. It was my first real glimpse into her haunted face unhinged.

FRENCH EDUCATION

The heat that Sunday summer in Aix,
before you knew that I loved you.
I met you for lunch in a long red dress,
and you said I looked like a Victorian painting.

We sat next to the Fontaine des Quatre-Dauphins
and ate purple olives and loaves of hard bread.
We smeared them with cheese that smelled like sex.
At least that was how I imagined it.

Over sweating glasses of milky Pastis,
you handed me a list of books to read.
Proust, Breton, Duras, and Gide.
To complete my French education.

The heat that Sunday summer in Aix,
before you knew that I loved you.
Before you unzipped my long red dress.
Before I seduced you, after French class.

DEAR LANA:

You are the goddess of summertime sadness.
When mine hits, I play *The Paradise Edition* every week,
with "Gods & Monsters" on repeat.

When you said *God's Dead,*
I turned to the spiritual *Violet* you penned
not quite a Bible, but on a random, unnumbered page I read

I believe in the goodness in me.

DEAR TOPPS COMPANY:

I would like you to know that I grew into my Garbage Pail Kids name.

And that, in case of a fire, my GPK collection is one of the few things I plan to take with me.

And when I evacuated for Hurricane Irma one summer, I grabbed 6 material possessions:

- my purse
- my photo album
- my first teddy bear
- a safe with important documents
- my deceased mother's jewelry
- and my collection of GPK cards.

I would like R.L. Stine (aka R.L. Slime) to know that I'm no middle-grader, but I got goosebumps when I cracked open *Welcome to Smellville*.

It's now on my bookshelf—displayed prominently—among my not-so-juvenile (and not-so-gross) poetry books.

I guess you could say I'm still an '80s kid, and I'm nostalgic for the '80s.

I would also like you to know that I own the GPK movie and the cartoon series.

And that, at the height of the pandemic, I tried to dig them out of storage to re-watch them.

They were under too many heavy boxes to get to, and I was tired, so I settled for my new GPK book and stickers.

It was good to see my old friends Adam Bomb, Babbling Brooke, Brainy Janey, Cranky Frankie, Handy Sandy, Junkfood John, Luke Puke, Nervous Rex, Rob Slob and Wacky Jackie.

Thank you for the trip down memory lane and for some new GPK goods to look forward to.

Yours Truly,

Nutty Nicole

AURORA STARR SAYS...

my guardian angels are upset right now. They are weeping tears of sorrow. And she is so distressed by this, she just had to email me right away. She says it's time I ask for assistance from the realms. She says Archangel Ausiel stands ready to guide me toward my divine soul purpose. And Archangel Gabriel will help me conquer the self-doubts that are holding me back from sharing my gifts with the world. Aurora Starr says this celestial intervention is available now, and I must act quickly—to lock in the low introductory price of $14.99. I ignore Aurora Starr. Aurora Starr writes again. She says I'm in danger. I ignore Aurora Starr. Aurora Starr still does not like this. She sends another email, this time, with the subject line: *What's wrong with you Nicole?* I delete it unread.

RED TIDE

On my morning walk, I pass by houses on stilts, sweat in a summer sun hotter than I can remember. I pick up piles of plastic, bury belly-up fish released by the ocean in high sighs. I pray for the strength of the cordoned squares safeguarding a sea turtle's nest and the wooden crutches propping up a dying palm. I praise the salted air I can still breathe in and out freely. I praise this city that keeps giving despite our abuse.

CITY OF HOPE

This city seeps hope—
a stitched wound that heals after each rainy season.
In the neon pink sky and the electric blue of the ocean,
each day gives rise, ebb and flow
to the hustle for more and more.
But what is more?

If it's traffic, noise, pollution
it's less.
We want less.
And in the moments we grow tired of chasing excess
we summon the mourning doves that call
at night, in the starry heat, beckoning the slowdown.

In these moments, we too take our time,
tend to those who struggle,
those with lives grown too heavy.
We carry someone else's bag of groceries.
We gift fruit from our backyards.
We buy a colada to share—a Miami form of giving.

EPILOGUE

(SHORT) LOVE POEM FOR MIAMI

I love the sideways rain in April.
I love the jungle heat of July.

I love when the days and nights blush pinker.
I love how everyone escapes inside.

I love the turquoise of the ocean.
I love Versace's pool on Ocean Drive.

I love my mojitos with extra mint.
I love my ceviche with extra lime.

I love sharing a colada with colleagues.
I love how the cicadas staccato time.

I love the neon green iguanas.
I love the mangoes polka-dotting the sky.

I love the manatees moving slowly.
I love Miami's year-round natural high.

(LONG) LOVE POEM FOR MIAMI

I love that Miami is sexy and isn't afraid to seduce you.

I love how Nochebuena is a bigger celebration here than Christmas Day.

I love watching the fireworks from my poolside balcony the day after my birthday.

I love how mango and avocado season encourage people to share.

I love sharing a colada with colleagues.

I love the joy people take in watching me try new local dishes for the first time.

I love watching the moon with M from our balcony.

I love The Standard Hotel and the fire pit there the most.

I love how I first met Gloria Estefan at The Freedom Tower.

I love that Sofía Vergara travels to Miami often and that one day I may meet her.

I love that I've slept in the same house as Madonna, Elton John, and Princess Di.

I love the pool at Casa Casuarina.

I love that there's a brand new Maserati, Porsche, Range Rover, Rolls Royce and a Corvette parked near my 2011 Mustang in my apartment building's garage.

I love Le Chat Noir that unfortunately closed down.

I love the ritual of happy hour on Thursdays.

I love that I got to edit a Golden Girls zine from Miami.

I love The Golden Girls shirt that my friend L bought me one year for my birthday.

I love that it took me moving here to realize that The Golden Girls house is a historical landmark in Los Angeles, not Miami.

I love that Blanche couldn't have accepted Harry's proposal at the actual Joe's Stone Crab either.

I love lobster and stone crab season, and especially the stone crab from Joe's.

I love that I live where many vacation, although Tourist Season exhausts me.

I love Miami Spice and Spa Month.

I love the peacocks in Coconut Grove, and mostly because I don't have to live next to them.

I love the Main Library, and that there are 50 libraries in the County system.

I love the Gesu Church and how it makes me feel pure for a few brief moments.

I love that I can swim in the ocean any month of the year, although I usually choose not to.

I love Celia Cruz and "La vida es un carnival" especially.

I love the extravagant brunch at Zuma.

I love the Curtiss Mansion, Deering Estate, and Vizcaya.

I love that I saw Britney's come back performance at Mansion.

I love The Savoy Hotel.

I love drinks at Dirty French.

I love the duck and the sommelier at Boulud Sud.

I love that there's a restaurant here called Sexy Fish.

I love the cathedral of trees in Coconut Grove.

I love the fancy houses in Coco Plum.

I love the doctor who once showed me his private Salvador Dalí collection.

I love that I can't remember his name, but know I have his business card somewhere.

I love that I've lived (and traveled) enough places to forget some people's names.

I love that I can hear planes flying overhead.

I love that I can see cruise ships from my pool deck, even though I don't love most cruises.

I love the giant red sparkly *Moët & Chandon* bottle on the Scarlet Lady.

I love that there's a store called *Ñooo! QUE BARATO!*

I love Brickell Key and that there's only one way to get there.

I love the women who wear boots when the temperature dips below 70.

I love the people who wear all black in the hottest months.

I love that Unbranded has a guava wheat beer.

I love that Gianni's has a $24 margarita with flakes of 24-karat gold.

I love that my partner ordered it for me for my birthday.

I love that I didn't love the taste of it because that would have been an expensive habit.

I love that my colleagues bought me an inflatable deer for my birthday.

I love the plaster deer head hanging on my office wall.

I love how Fi'lia fills the streets with the smell of wood-burning fire.

I love Brew at the Zoo and that the one time I went, I got to see Flock of Seagulls play there.

I love the Fillmore because Tori Amos has her concerts there.

I love the ice rink at the Intercontinental and that it's only operational around Christmas.

I love the key lime pie from Publix.

I love Seasons 52 because their menu changes with the seasons even though Miami doesn't.

I love having cocktails at The Four Seasons in Brickell.

I love that J.Lo and Shakira performed at Super Bowl LIV when Miami hosted.

I love that I turned down free tickets because I'm ethical.

I love Fairchild Garden and their jazz concerts under the moon.

I love when my hairdresser paints my hair like a canvas.

I love the word *balayage*.

I love the rainy season most.

I love the French Consulate Office on Brickell Avenue.

I love the old Tobacco Road.

I love everyone who has tried to teach me how to Salsa.

I love that Manolo & Rene and Caffe Tonny are open 24 hours.

I love the girl who comes home from the club as I head to work in the morning.

I love the pianist who lives across the hall from me.

I love that I don't know what she looks like.

I love that I'd only know her by sound.

I love the people at the front desk who say good morning, good afternoon, and good evening, regardless of how they are feeling.

I love the hustle of the people who slide their business cards under my door.

I love the people who scent the elevator with fresh lavender or pine.

I love that given the choice, I chose the South Tower over the North.

I love the person who taught me the word *putica*.

I love that I thought it was the word for a doll.

I love that it is only the letter n that separates the words *bridge* and *whore* in Spanish.

I love that I accidentally confused them at work, but only once.

I love that Miami feels so different from the rest of the South.

I love taking the train to feel a sense of adventure.

I love the pasta and the atmosphere at Soya y Pomodoro.

I love that my job involves both poetry and policy.

I love that I've said gay 13 times in this book now.

I love anyone who defends that right.

I love the people who will buy this book anyway.

I love the people who will buy extra copies because of it.

I love the famous people I see out and about, but am too shy to approach.

I love that Miami's soccer team wears pink jerseys and that the football team wears aqua.

I love that our mascots are a dolphin named T.D., a marlin named Billy, a Kingfisher named Golazo, and a fireball named Burnie.

I love that LeBron James once lived in my building.

I love the ladies who practically fainted when David Beckham paid a visit to our office.

I love that people have mostly stopped asking where I'm from after more than a decade of living in Miami.

I love the women who wear stilettos for just about everything.

I love that no one wears pantyhose here.

I love that *gordo* is a term of endearment.

I love the guy who walks his three dachshunds every morning.

I love that I've never heard him talk.

I love that the mail ladies have my apartment number memorized and recognize me by face.

I love that they call me the book and wine lady.

I love the landlords who don't gauge their tenants.

I love the New Yorkers who don't drive up my rent.

I love The Writer's Room at The Betsy Hotel.

I love the idea of hosting three martini afternoons at The Betsy.

I love the perfume at Alberto Cortes.

I love that there's both a Ross and a CVS in my building.

I love Lapis at the Fontainebleau.

I love all of the authors who come to Book Fair each November.

I love Miami Book Fair and The Miami International Film Festival.

I love Books & Books.

I love O, Miami.

I love our First Madam Mayor.

I love that Dolly Parton hosted a New Year's Eve bash here.

I love that Gloria Estefan, Jennifer Lopez, and several Real Housewives have houses on Star Island.

I love that Oprah has a penthouse on Fisher Island.

I love that Cher and Matt Damon own property on La Gorce Island.

I love that there are many other celebrities on Sunset and Indian Creek Island.

I love that I met Isabelle Hubert in Miami and that she was cold.

I love that she kind of ghosted the official Film Festival after-party.

I love staying mostly indoors July, August and September while most of the world is enjoying summer.

I love that the Versace mansion was once an apartment complex for artists.

I love that the original owner may have had an undercover gay lover.

I love that the official paperwork lists this potential lover as an adopted "son."

I love that my partner always finds a place in our small, but cozy apartment for all the books I bring home.

I love my crew at *South Florida Poetry Journal*.

I love the ladies of *SWWIM*.

I love the mourning dove that wakes me each morning.

I love the cicadas that sing me to sleep at night.

I love seeing Pink Martini every time they perform at The Arsht Center.

I love the Frost Museum and the PAMM.

I love listening to jazz on Sundays thanks to DJ Swanky.

I love everyone who supports the arts.

I love our local historian, Dr. Paul George.

I love being only a 4-hour drive from The Hemingway and Bishop House.

I love the few people who actually use turn signals and yield to incoming traffic.

I love the soup my partner makes me every week night, even in the heat of summer.

I love the photo I took of the Brigitte Bardot mural in Wynwood.

I love that Whole Foods and SILVERSPOT are all within walking distance from my building.

I love the trees and walking paths at Simpson Park.

I love the doorman, Fernando, who passed away not too long ago.

I love how people still call me miss when I'm wearing extra-large sunglasses.

I love my Miami family.

I love how nostalgic I get for Michigan when I'm in Miami and vice versa.

I love that the last fancy dinner I had with my mother was at Tuyo, and that I was able to treat her to the very best.

I love that Richard Blanco is our Poet Laureate.

I love being our County's Poetry Ambassador.

I love the Miami poets and think we need our own school.

I love seeing Miami through both local and tourist eyes.

I love when people think I don't understand Spanish, and the things I get to overhear as a result.

I love everyone who adds to this poem.

VERSACE

Versace died more than 25 years ago in Miami.
Versace's home is now a hotel.
(Two people stayed the night and killed themselves there).
(Madonna, Elton John, and Princess Di also spent the night there).
Versace's observatory is neglected.
VERSACE is as relevant as ever.
(Britney wore VERSACE to her recent wedding.)
Versace is the title of a song by Migos.
Versace sang Miami's praises.
Versace said Miami is simple and beautiful.
Versace would be surprised to see Miami now.
Versace may also be surprised by his latest designs.
Versace designs yoga pants from the dead.
VERSACE yoga pants are $975.
VERSACE has an online authentication system.
VERSACE wants you to help fight counterfeiting.
VERSACE does not want you to buy FERSACE™.
VERSACE wants you to wear the real VERSACE.
VERSACE also designs dry-clean jeans.
Versace said don't be into trends.
Versace died way too soon.
VERSACE is Miami.
Versace, Miami misses you.

ACKNOWLEDGMENTS

I am grateful to the editors of the following publications where some of these poems will soon appear or first appeared, at times in earlier versions: *Pidgeonholes*, *Gulf Stream Magazine*, *Whale Road Review*, *The Broadkill Review*, *The Bear River Review*, *Maudlin House*, *HAD*, *trampset*, *Identity Theory*, *The Daily Drunk*, *Wine Cellar Press*, *Stone of Madness Press*, *Cultural Daily*, *warning lines magazine*, *SWWIM*, *The Hallowzine*, *Emerge Literary Journal*, *Final Girl Bulletin Board*, *Roi Fainéant Press*, *CLOVES Literary*, *The Hungry Ghost Project*, *Hello America Stereo Cassette*, *the winnow*, *theVERSEverse*, *The TICKLE*, *Limp Wrist*, *Olney*, *The Coop*, PIANO SLAM's newsletter, Jason Novak's Twitter cartoon illustrations, O, Miami's "Portrait at 34," *It Came From Beneath the Ink! An R.L. Stine Tribute Anthology* (edited by Lannie Stabile), *The Alien Buddha's House of Horrors 4* (edited by Red Focks), *Dreams & Nightmares* (edited by Aura Martin), *HELL IS REAL: A Midwest Gothic Anthology* (edited by Jack Apollo Hartley), *The Midnight Mass Anthology (*edited by Rachael Crosbie and Charlie D'Aniello Trigueros*)*, *Marvelous Verses (*edited by Jared Beloff*)*, *Be Kind Rewind* (edited by Casey Dawson), *Hello, How Can I Help You Today* (edited by Casey Dawson), and *Let Me Say This: A Dolly Parton Poetry Anthology* (edited by Julie E. Bloemeke and Dustin Brookshire).

So that I don't risk plagiarizing myself, I will also acknowledge that some of the poems in this book were published in different versions in *Poems for the People* (The Southern Collective Experience Press, February 2023), and I am grateful to Clifford Brooks III for giving those poems a home as well.

I am grateful to all my poet friends and especially to those who have provided feedback on the poems that make up this manuscript, including Maureen Seaton, Jared Beloff, and Adrian Dallas Frandle.

For this book, I specifically wanted blurbs from poets with Miami ties, and I am grateful to Richard Blanco, Denise Duhamel, Ariel Francisco, Caridad Moro-Gronlier, and

Maureen Seaton for writing such beautiful and thoughtful blurbs for *FERSACE*.

I am grateful to my partner, Militza, and all of my non-poet friends and family for supporting my work.

I am grateful to Miami and Michigan, my two polar-opposite "homes" for providing an abundance of inspiration.

I am grateful to you for reading *FERSACE*. Thank you! Please continue to read more living poets, along with the dead. We're in conversation with each other.

NOTES

The epigraph for *FERSACE* comes from a 1994 PBS interview between Gianni Versace and Charlie Rose.

In my poems, Versace refers to the person (Gianni Versace) and VERSACE refers to the brand. I chose to capitalize FERSACE for consistency with my capitalization of the VERSACE brand.

"Not Seen," "TOO DARK (Part I)," "The Future," and "Not Clear" were all written in collaboration with a Ouija board.

"Fall" is styled after several poems in Victoria Chang's *Obit*.

"Rifle Season" is for the soft boys.

"Mami," "Flaca," and "Gringa" are haiku written in response to various names I've been called in Miami versus Michigan. I love this form for its brevity, mystery, 3-line 5-7-5 syllable count, and its frequent seasonal references.

"A Woman Called My Face" was inspired by Kamilah Aisha Moon's "Portrait at 34." This poem is for her and for my mother, Nancy.

"Hemingway Drank Mojitos and Other Miami Myths" is a semi-cento and was inspired by articles written by Philip Greene for *Eater* and Connie Ogle for *The Miami Herald*.

"Fake Plastic Trees" borrows its title from the Radiohead song of the same name.

"Winter" is for everyone who loves the cold, for the people who have tried to escape it, and for everyone looking for "home."

"Cloud on My Tongue" is a villanelle, a form that lends itself to music, and it borrows its title from the Tori Amos song of the same name, along with the line "All the girls here are freezing cold." This poem is for Tori and for the amazing people at the 2023 Dranoff 2 Piano Foundation's PIANO SLAM.

The line "Can you believe that some of your fans take a trip to Indiana just to see your braid?" in "Dear Sylvia:" was inspired by Diane Seuss' "Self-Portrait with Sylvia Plath's Braid." This poem is for Sylvia.

"Dear Gianni:" is written for Gianni Versace.

"Dear Betty:" is written for Betty White.

In order of appearance, "Cento for 17 Mutuals" borrows lines from poems in *Emerge Literary Journal* by: Samantha DeFlitch ("Dogs on the Roof," Issue 19); Jared Beloff ("Living Happily at the End of the World," Issue 20); Madeleine Corley ("Theft," Issue 16); Lannie Stabile ("brother, brother, brother," Issue 18); Cyndie Randall ("Your Dreams and Your Light Are Too Ordinary, My Love," Issue 18); Francine Witte ("Why Do You Ask?," Issue 12); Lynne Schmidt ("Learning German," Issue 19); Andrew Bertaina ("In Spain," Issue 20); Aleah Dye ("Body Heat," Issue 15); Rachael Crosbie ("Versions of Fire," Issue 17); C. Cimmone ("Chains," Issue 20); Damian Rucci ("In Places Like This," Issue 16); Ayesha Asad ("Teatime and Boiled Ginger," Issue 13); Lindsey Heatherly ("Routine," Issue 14); Danielle Rose ("Diving," Issue 17); Leigh Chadwick ("Author Writes About Herself in the Third Person or: The Poem of Tiny Clouds," Issue 20); Andrew Bertaina ("In Spain," Issue 20); Marissa Glover ("Homeland," Issue 16). This poem is for them.

"Summer" is for my Grandma Gladys Tallman.

"The Velvet Room" is for Richie Hofmann, who supplied the prompt that inspired this poem.

"Pay the poets!" is for all the poets.

"The moon is gay (aka Say Gay!)" is for all LGBTQ+ readers. I learned after writing this poem that J. Jennifer Espinoza has a poem called "The Moon is Trans," and that seems like a strong possibility too. This poem also borrows lyrics from "Starlite-Rainbow Bright" from the Rainbow Brite Album "Paint A Rainbow In Your Heart."

"Blank Space" borrows its title and italicized content from Taylor Swift's song of the same name. This poem is for Taylor and for Amy Long.

"Dear Lana:" borrows wording from Lana Del Rey's song "Gods & Monsters." This poem is for Lana.

"Aurora Starr says…" borrows lines from emails sent to me by Aurora Starr.

"Red Tide" is for all marine life.

"City of Hope" is for Mayor Daniella Levine Cava and the residents of Miami-Dade County.

"(Short) Love Poem for Miami" and "(Long) Love Poem for Miami" are written for the City of Miami. They are inspired by Alex Dimitrov's poem "Love."

"VERSACE" is for Gianni Versace.

ABOUT THE AUTHOR

Nicole Tallman is the author of three collections: *Something Kindred* (The SCE Press, 2022), *Poems for the People* (The SCE Press, 2023), and *FERSACE*. A Michigan native, she lives in Miami and serves as the official Poetry Ambassador for Miami-Dade County. Find her on social media @natallman and at nicoletallman.com

Headshot courtesy of Glamour Shots, 1994.